MW01121479

The Plum Tree

by Mitch Miyagawa

The Truth.
Lies.
Buried.

The Plum Tree

by

Mitch Miyagawa

Playwrights Canada Press

Playwrights Canada Press
215 Spadina Ave. Suite 230, Toronto, Ontario CANADA M5T 2C7
416.703.0013 fax 416.408.3402
orders@playwrightscanada.com • www.playwrightscanada.com

Playwrights Canada Press acknowledges the support of the taxpayers of Canada and the province of Ontario through The Canada Council for the Arts and the Ontario Arts Council.

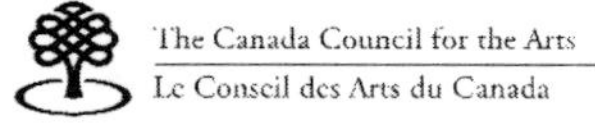

Cover design and image by Tanya Handley.
Production Editor: Mirka Zivanovic-Kosciuk

National Library of Canada Cataloguing in Publication

Mitch Miyagawa
The plum tree / Mitch Miyagawa.

A play.
ISBN 0-88754-736-2

1. Japanese Canadians—Evacuation and relocation, 1942-1945—Drama. I. Title.

PS8576.I898P58 2004 C812'.6 C2004-900363-1

First edition: April 2004.
Printed and bound by Printco at Toronto, Canada.

for Dad, and all my aunts and uncles

Acknowledgements

My sincere thanks to Michael Clark and Nakai Theatre, Patti Fraser, Stephen Hill, Marcus Youssef, Ben Henderson, Patti Flather, Jared Matsunaga-Turnbull, Jovanni Sy, Mary Sloan, John Murrell, Rachel Henessey, Canada Council for the Arts Quest Program, Yukon Advanced Artist Award, Lise-Ann Johnson, Brian Parkinson, Vanessa Porteous, Bob White and Alberta Theatre Projects, Hiro Kanagawa, Darcy Dunlop, Sarah Stanley, Donna Spencer and Firehall Theatre, Adrienne Wong, and Angela Walkley.

The Playwright acknowledges the assistance of the 2001 and 2002 Banff playRites Colony - a partnership between the Canada Council for the Arts, The Banff Centre for the Arts, and Alberta Theatre Projects.

The Plum Tree was workshopped and received a public reading as part of the National Arts Centre (Ottawa) English Theatre On the Verge Theatre New Works Festival 2002. It was also part of the University of Lethbridge's Canadian Plays In Development workshop in June 2002.

Production History

The Plum Tree was originally produced in Whitehorse, Yukon at Nakai Theatre, from March 22 - 30, 2002, with the following cast:

GEORGE	Jared Matsunaga-Turnbull
FRIEDA	Mary Sloan
MAS	Jovanni Sy
Director:	Michael Clark
Set / Costume Designer:	David Skelton
Sound Designer:	Daniel Janke
Light Designer:	Craig Moddle
Stage Manager:	Dean Eyre

A subsequent revised version of *The Plum Tree* was produced in Calgary, Alberta at Alberta Theatre Projects' National playRites Festival, January 22 - March 2, 2003, with the following cast:

GEORGE	Jared Matsunaga-Turnbull
FRIEDA	Darcy Dunlop
MAS	Hiro Kanagawa
Director:	Sarah Stanley
Set/Prop Designer:	Scott Reid
Costume Designer:	Jen Darbellay
Sound Designer:	Kevin McGugan
Light Designer:	Terry Middleton
Production Dramaturg:	Vanessa Porteous
Assistant Dramaturg:	Vicki Stroich
Production Stage Manager:	Dianne Goodman
Stage Manager:	Rhonda Kambeitz
Assistant Stage Manager:	Kelly Lunn

Characters

GEORGE MURAKAMI, 32. Japanese-Canadian.

FRIEDA WAGNER, 68. German-Canadian.

MAS MURAKAMI, 60. Japanese-Canadian. George's uncle. Spirit.

Setting

A U-Pick berry farm near Mission, BC, Canada, 1989. A clearing between the farmhouse and the plum tree.

ACT ONE, SCENE ONE

Mid-morning. MAS sits in the tree. GEORGE enters the clearing. He does not see MAS.

MAS Boo!

GEORGE God!

MAS Got ya.

GEORGE Uncle?

MAS Surprised to see me, eh?

GEORGE Just a little.

MAS comes down from the tree.

I've dreamt about you. Waiting here for me.

MAS Here I am.

GEORGE Here you are. Is Dad…

MAS You think he'd be hanging around here?

GEORGE Guess not.

MAS C'mon, George. Here we are. Together. We always talked about coming here. Remember?

GEORGE It doesn't look like the photo.

MAS Falling apart. All overgrown.

Pause.

GEORGE What.

MAS There's the door, nephew. You remember how to knock.

FRIEDA enters. She sees GEORGE and picks up a shovel.

FRIEDA Hey. Hey!

GEORGE Oh. Hello.

FRIEDA What do you think you're doing?

GEORGE There was no one here so I thought —

FRIEDA — thought you'd snoop around a little?

GEORGE No, in fact, I / wanted to —

FRIEDA / does this look like the kind of place you can just start picking berries?

GEORGE Your sign says U-Pick, doesn't it?

MAS Just tell her, George.

FRIEDA I wasn't expecting any customers today. Should've worn gumboots.

GEORGE What?

FRIEDA It's rained every day this week, you know. You drove out from Vancouver.

GEORGE Yes, but I don't—

FRIEDA — drove straight out to my U-Pick. Just woke up this morning and thought, my goodness, I could use a bucket of raspberries. Better wear my best shoes.

MAS Listen to her!

FRIEDA And rental plates, too.

GEORGE I flew in this morning, actually. From Winnipeg.

FRIEDA Even better.

GEORGE I've got business in the area.

FRIEDA Business.

GEORGE Research. I research —

FRIEDA — oh, I see, research. That's a new one. Snooping around. Seeing how your new strip mall would fit? If you're interested in the Open House, just say so.

GEORGE Open House.

FRIEDA Yes, Open House. As if you didn't know.

GEORGE I didn't know. Really. There's no sign.

FRIEDA There was an ad in the paper.

GEORGE I told you. I flew in from Winnipeg this morning. Look. I have a card. I'm a researcher.

FRIEDA *(squinting at card)* Grudge.

GEORGE George.

FRIEDA Hmf. Frieda Wagner. This is difficult for me. People coming and going all the time.

GEORGE You've had a lot of interest in the house?

FRIEDA I'm not going to sell to just anyone. They've got to have the proper appreciation. Not some vulture from the city out to make a fast buck. They all think I'm just a helpless old lady.

GEORGE I'm sure they don't think that.

FRIEDA Kept the place up by myself for ten years. And look at it.

GEORGE I'd like to.

FRIEDA What?

GEORGE I'd like to look at it. The inside.

FRIEDA Why?

GEORGE For professional reasons. I'm doing historical research. And this house is obviously – historical.

FRIEDA I have a lot of work to do.

FRIEDA enters the house and closes the door.

MAS I don't believe you, nephew. "Historical research".

GEORGE You saw how suspicious she was. I had to say something.

MAS Shoulda just been straight. We're samurai. Warriors.

GEORGE Oh, God.

MAS Come on. Go in there and tell her.

GEORGE I'm doing this my way.

MAS Be straight! Samurai!

GEORGE If I was straight, she would think I was after something.

MAS You are.

GEORGE knocks on the door. FRIEDA answers.

GEORGE Did you have a garden here?

FRIEDA What?

GEORGE A garden.

FRIEDA Where.

GEORGE I don't know, by the plum tree maybe —

FRIEDA — Why would you ask a question like that?

GEORGE Just seems like it would be a nice spot for a garden. Close to the house.

FRIEDA No. There was nothing there.

MAS Yes, there was.

GEORGE You're sure.

FRIEDA What do you mean, am I sure? Of course I'm sure. It's my property.

MAS It was right there, George.

Sound of trains.

FRIEDA Day and night, that rail yard. You damned developers just want to take over the whole valley, bulldoze everything into the ground, plaster Chinese on some apartment building. Sometimes, your people, I don't know what they —

GEORGE — My people?

FRIEDA Your kind. Your — you know what I mean.

GEORGE I'm not Chinese.

FRIEDA Oh.

GEORGE I'm Japanese.

FRIEDA You have to go now.

GEORGE I'd like to pick some berries.

FRIEDA Fine. Just don't bother me.

FRIEDA slams the door.

Pause. Sound of rain.

MAS It always rains here.

GEORGE begins picking.

Jesus, George.

GEORGE I said I wanted to pick.

MAS When I was a kid, we picked so much, I couldn't stand the smell of raspberry jam.

GEORGE Just let me think for a minute.

MAS Dad used to have this old soya sauce container right here. Mom would put a buncha rice in it. Dad would come along with this big mallet. Wham! Mom would turn the rice with a stick. Wham! Wham! Eh? For *mochi*. What's wrong, George. How come you're afraid to use the mallet. You're a warrior.

GEORGE What's the point of being a warrior? What did I ever win?

MAS strikes a samurai pose.

What's that.

MAS "It is a job promising no pay or reward." Kambei Shimada. The grizzled veteran. "Seven Samurai?" C'mon. We watched that movie a million times.

GEORGE You talked about this place all the time. And you never came back. I did.

MAS And how come it took you so long?

GEORGE I was busy.

MAS Scared of what your Dad might think? Scared he might give you the ol' Frank silent treatment?

GEORGE I wasn't scared.

MAS Oh, I know, George. I saw you slam your head against that wall. It was painful to watch. "Hey Dad, I started organizing meetings" "Hey Dad, would you sign this Redress petition?" "Aren't you proud of me, Dad?" Nothing. Stone wall Frank. Well, nothing to worry about now, eh?

GEORGE Uncle. I'm doing this my way.

MAS Gonna be a wet way. All right then. Let's see what you got.

Pause. GEORGE goes to the door and knocks. FRIEDA answers.

FRIEDA What is it.

GEORGE I picked some berries.

FRIEDA Twenty dollars a bucket.

GEORGE I haven't picked much. Wrong shoes.

FRIEDA Half a bucket is twelve.

GEORGE I've only got a twenty.

FRIEDA *(taking money)* That will do.

GEORGE About your Open House.

FRIEDA The Open House is over. Paper printed the wrong address.

GEORGE Well, if you'd like to talk to me about the house sometime, I'll give you my / card, and—

FRIEDA *(not taking card)*/ is there something in your ears? I told you. I'm very busy.

GEORGE Fine.

GEORGE turns to leave.

FRIEDA Why are you so interested in this house?

GEORGE I told you. I research old houses.

FRIEDA You save these houses.

GEORGE It depends on their — historical significance.

FRIEDA And this house?

GEORGE It's a beautiful place.

FRIEDA You think so.

GEORGE Roof needs some work.

FRIEDA Henry promised to look at it.

GEORGE Your husband.

FRIEDA No. My son. My husband had a bad arm from the war, he could never fix that roof. So you think the house is maybe…

GEORGE I'd have to know more about it. Who built it.

MAS Jesus, George, will you just tell / her —

GEORGE / and if there are any significant artefacts. Historical objects.

MAS Ah, so. Very sly.

FRIEDA We were immigrants, too, you know, my husband and I, just like your parents.

MAS Immigrants.

GEORGE My parents were born in Canada.

FRIEDA Yes, well, you know what I mean. My husband has been dead now for ten years. I kept the place up myself. Henry would help, but he's so busy. I work hard, you know. I know it doesn't look like much, but / I —

GEORGE / like I said, it's a beautiful place.

Pause.

FRIEDA This work you do. Who is it for.

GEORGE The Historical Preservation Committee. Of Mission City. The Mission City Historical Preservation Committee.

MAS The what?

GEORGE Committee's very interested in Japanese homes around here. Used to be a big community here, before the war.

FRIEDA The war was so terrible. Ordinary people had to do terrible things. We heard about what happened, how your people were, what do you call it…

MAS Trucked out like cattle. Thrown in jail.

GEORGE Evacuated.

FRIEDA Yes. I'm sure whoever it was, the people in government, they had no choice.

MAS You ignorant / kraut.

GEORGE / if, say, Japanese owned this house at some point, or if there were any artefacts, it might add to the historical significance of the house. The Committee would make a very generous donation.

FRIEDA Goodbye.

GEORGE But —

FRIEDA — I have to go. I have a meeting with my sister in town. Here is your money back. Keep the berries. They are almost rotten anyway.

FRIEDA slams the door.

ACT ONE, SCENE TWO

Late afternoon. GEORGE and MAS in the clearing.

MAS She's not here. Get that shovel. Come on. She could come back any second.

GEORGE gets shovel.

GEORGE Where?

MAS What do you mean, where? By the plum tree.

GEORGE There's a lot of places by the plum tree.

MAS I only told you a million times where they were.

GEORGE You'd only say, in the garden, right by the plum tree. She said there was no garden.

MAS Here.

GEORGE Rock.

MAS Over there.

GEORGE Too many roots.

MAS These goddamned berry bushes. Grow like weeds if you don't control 'em. Old lady really let this place fall apart. I thought "her people" were always tidy. "They had no choice." Gimme a break.

GEORGE It's not her fault.

MAS She was going to take a swing at you with that shovel. This would just be a lot easier if you would just ask the old bag.

GEORGE Think of this as a sneak attack.

MAS Sneak attack. More like don't rock the boat. *Shikataga-nai*, eh, George? Same old bull.

GEORGE Three years. I did my time.

MAS So why stop now.

GEORGE Because I'm tired of pushing. Remember those two old Nakashimas on their farm? I showed them a picture of their fishing boat. They both started crying. Old guys had probably never cried in their lives. They were so ashamed.

MAS 'Cause they never stood up for themselves. I could see my family all lined up over there, waiting for that train. Police were stomping around in the bushes. Never woulda found me, up in this tree. But then I hear Frank. "I know the trails. I'll show you where he is." My own brother. Plucked me right out of this tree.

GEORGE He was worried.

MAS He was scared. Scared my trouble would come down on him.

GEORGE puts the shovel by the house.

GEORGE And the family. He didn't want you to break up the family.

MAS He broke it anyway. Sent me straight out to Angler. Wasn't like those cushy camps in the mountains. Guys with guns. Uniforms.

Pause.

We buried them the day before that. They were so beautiful. Golden crane painted on each one. Mom kept them so polished. "Mas," she said. "Go help your brother pack up that old rhubarb crate. "

FRIEDA enters. She puts bags of groceries in front of the door and notices GEORGE. She grabs the shovel.

Your grandpa said, "Ah, why bother, we'll be back in a month, two maybe " but Mom said, "Go get the shovel."

FRIEDA takes a swing at GEORGE and hits him in the arm. She swings again.

GEORGE Wait —

FRIEDA — Get off my land!

MAS It's war, George!

FRIEDA My land, you hear!

MAS You gotta fight. You got no choice. Samurai!

GEORGE Stop!

GEORGE grabs the shovel.

FRIEDA I'm calling the police.

GEORGE Stop!

GEORGE grabs FRIEDA.

I forgot my umbrella. I came back to get it.

FRIEDA Your umbrella.

GEORGE I left it here when I was picking berries.

FRIEDA You frightened me. I didn't think. I just — I don't know who you are. Are you — ?

GEORGE You almost broke my arm.

FRIEDA I'm — I'm — let me look at it.

GEORGE I'm fine.

FRIEDA Please. It's not so bad is it. I'm just an old lady after all.

Short pause.

The funny thing is that I was wishing you had left me your card.

GEORGE Why.

FRIEDA Would you like to come in.

GEORGE No. That's fine.

Pause.

FRIEDA I wanted to talk to you about your work. With this committee. And this house. Supposing this was a — historic house.

GEORGE Supposing.

FRIEDA There were Japanese here before the war. We… heard about it from the neighbours.

GEORGE Was there / anything —

FRIEDA / it's my sister. She says I can't take care of the place. And now she's given me a week.

GEORGE For what.

FRIEDA To sell. Or she'll knock it down. Liesel, my own sister! My own family. Crackers. I bought some, won't / you —

GEORGE / no. Thank you.

FRIEDA It's more for Henry than for me. He still needs a place to call home. Can your committee help me?

GEORGE Do what.

FRIEDA I don't know, some kind of protection, something so no one could knock it down, so it would stay the same.

GEORGE The place needs a lot of work. To get it up to the committee's standards.

FRIEDA You think that it's possible.

GEORGE Anything's possible.

Short pause.

FRIEDA Maybe you could stay for supper. So we could talk more. About — possibilities.

MAS Just tell her.

GEORGE All right.

FRIEDA Good. Well. What will I cook? I just bought a roast, in case Henry came back tonight but I think he will not come tonight. Where is your car? I didn't see it.

GEORGE I parked up the road.

FRIEDA Oh?

GEORGE So I could walk here. See all the other properties around here.

FRIEDA Perhaps you can go for a walk back in the trails. They go all the way down to the rail yard. If you wish, you can use Henry's boots. I will make us a plum pie!

ACT ONE, SCENE THREE

Early evening. After supper.

FRIEDA More pie?

GEORGE No. Thank you.

MAS Isn't this nice George. How's those plums taste?

GEORGE You're just like my grandmother.

MAS Your Grandma made wine with those plums. Her plums.

l to r: Jared Matsunaga-Turnbull, Hiro Kanagawa, Darcy Dunlop

photo by Trudie Lee

FRIEDA I ruined that roast. It was so salty.

GEORGE No, no. It was delicious.

FRIEDA You're so skinny. Doesn't your wife feed you?

MAS What's Susan up to now, anyway?

GEORGE She's not much of a cook.

MAS Your grandma was a good cook.

FRIEDA Henry and I, we always have a good meal when he comes home. I guess he will not make it tonight. It's important for families to eat together.

MAS Ah, family. Used to set the table special at New Year's, George.

FRIEDA Give me your plate.

MAS Mom kept our plates so polished. It was like those cranes were on fire. Tell her.

GEORGE Here. Let me help you.

FRIEDA No, no.

GEORGE Please.

MAS "Let me help you. Please." I'm a very patient person. You know that. I can sit for hours. Hell, that's all we did in Angler Camp.

FRIEDA Look at this place. Why I bother.

GEORGE Why do you?

FRIEDA What.

GEORGE Why do you stay.

FRIEDA My walks in the woods. I don't know. Sometimes I go walking at night. I can see the lights of the house through the woods. Waiting for me. *(getting picture from pocket)* Look. Werner and I at the train station the day we left Meissen. I am very fat. Pregnant and happy. It was one of the happiest days of my life. I still think of it, when I hear those trains.

Pause.

Meissen was all — broken stones. It's all done now.

GEORGE It's history.

FRIEDA That's right.

GEORGE That's what my father always used to say. It's history, George. Meaning — don't make a fuss. Erase it. But you can't.

FRIEDA Your father had the right idea.

GEORGE My father! My father didn't really have ideas. No politics, no talking about issues. Hated it when I got involved in the — we'd argue all the time. Until he just — stopped talking. That's the way he was.

MAS The Clam King, that Frank.

GEORGE My uncle, on the other hand. A real inspiration. Started organizing, talking about getting something back for what happened in the war. No one would listen to him. Said there'd be backlash. Turned their backs on him.

FRIEDA There was an apology from the government. I read it in the paper. Money and an apology.

GEORGE Yes.

FRIEDA Your family must have been happy.

MAS Buncha stones.

GEORGE They tend to be — reserved. It was painful. Brought back a lot of memories.

MAS Reserved! Buncha stones.

GEORGE They try to just erase the pain. They even have a saying for it. *Shikataga-nai*. "Nothing can be done."

MAS Bull.

FRIEDA But your uncle must have been happy. With what he got.

GEORGE No.

FRIEDA What more did he want?

GEORGE Something more personal. He's gone anyway. Lung cancer.

MAS lights a cigarette.

FRIEDA Let me give you something else. More coffee. Some cookies.

GEORGE No thank you. I think I should go.

FRIEDA Wait.

Pause.

This was our new life, you see? For us, for Henry. We had to practically start this farm again, rip everything up, and we found — this place was such a mess, especially between the house and the plum tree, where the garden was —

GEORGE — there was a garden.

FRIEDA I had forgotten. It was so long ago. I, I never wanted this place. But you have to understand. We had no choice. It was such a confusing time. That's why I want you to help me. To help me save it.

GEORGE Like I said. Maybe I can help.

FRIEDA You could talk to your committee.

GEORGE Yes. I could talk to them.

FRIEDA Thank you.

GEORGE You're welcome.

Pause.

I should go — I don't even have a hotel room yet.

FRIEDA Stay. Stay here. You can work from here.

GEORGE I don't know if I would feel right.

FRIEDA Please. You could stay in Henry's room.

MAS Frank's room. Your Dad's.

GEORGE All right.

FRIEDA Good. I'll go make up that room. Your wife won't be jealous, I hope.

GEORGE We're separated.

FRIEDA I'm sorry. I say such stupid things.

FRIEDA turns to go.

It might clear up tonight. We may even see the moon.

ACT ONE, SCENE FOUR

Night. Moonlight. A candle glows in the window of the house. Sound of trains. GEORGE is digging under the plum tree.

MAS That Kurosawa, eh, George? Wish we could watch that movie again. *(enacting "Seven Samurai")* The sixteenth century. An age of turbulence. Japan was in the throes of civil war. Farmers everywhere were being crushed under the iron heels of cruel marauders. *(imitating farmers)* Is there no God to protect us? Let's give everything to the invaders and then hang ourselves! *Shikataga-nai*! *(imitating Old Man)* Listen to me. You must hire samurai.

Enter — the two samurai. Me and my disciple. Out to save those poor farmers. And now. Weary from battle. We return. To find — it's all been taken away. Hidden. And so my disciple plans a sneak attack. And then — he eats pie. And when his attack is ready — he washes dishes. And to finish off the enemy — he goes to bed.

GEORGE Uncle.

MAS Eight of us lived in this little house. What's it like.

GEORGE The house?

MAS Yeah.

GEORGE It's very cozy.

MAS *(looking in window)* Really falling apart, huh.

GEORGE Wood in the ceiling is beautiful.

MAS Dad milled it himself.

GEORGE There's an old stove in the corner of the living room.

MAS Might be the same one we had. I can almost smell your *Oba-chan*'s salmon. What else?

GEORGE Bathroom is just off the kitchen.

MAS We had an old gasoline drum for a bath.

GEORGE And then the bedrooms are in the back.

MAS What's that room like? Frank never let us in there much. He got his own room because he was *nee-san*. Older brother.

GEORGE It's just a room. Why don't you go inside and look around.

MAS Nah. You know. Wouldn't really be the same.

GEORGE *(indicating hole)* Nothing.

MAS Keep going.

GEORGE There's nothing here.

MAS Maybe over / there.

GEORGE / there's nothing here.

GEORGE begins to put dirt back in the hole.

MAS How 'bout another story, George? How about Uncle Mas Goes To Camp? You always liked that one.

MAS climbs the tree halfway and throws plums at GEORGE.

You'll never get me, copper! Hay-ah! Take that! Shoulda seen them. Necks all purple. Got Frank square between the eyes. Heh. Then I tore up my ID card and threw it at their faces. But they dragged me out of this tree. Two weeks on a train to Ontario. Me and the rest of the resisters. Kid with a handful of fruit, a resister. We had to wear red circles on our backs, George. / So we were easier targets.

GEORGE *(simultaneously, as if he's heard the story a million times)* So you were easier targets.

MAS You remember! And then the big finale. One big bomb and… *(lobbing plum at GEORGE)* War's over, boys. "Our people" lost. Hooray. We're going home.

GEORGE Why didn't you ever come back here?

MAS Wouldn't let us. Wouldn't let us anywhere near the coast. We're island people. We need the ocean.

GEORGE They lifted the ban. But you never came back.

MAS It was stay out east or go back to Japan. "Go back", eh, George? Good joke. Most've us had never been there! So you know what we did. We went samurai. We attacked with the only thing we had. Our butts.

GEORGE *(simultaneously)* Your butts.

MAS We just sat on our butts for weeks. Refused to move, even after they closed the camp. But it was pointless. So I went out to Winnipeg. To my parents and brothers and sisters. The sheep. Your Dad, of course was the worst.

GEORGE You were pushy. You didn't know when to stop.

MAS Chicken-shit Frank.

GEORGE Stop it.

MAS Goddamned Frank —

GEORGE — Stop it!

MAS We played cowboys and indians in those trails. We fished for suckers in the creek. And he didn't lift a finger to get it back. To get anything back. What's enough for you, George. That's the question. Well. You know what they say. It's history.

GEORGE picks up the shovel to begin digging again. FRIEDA can be heard singing offstage. GEORGE hears and hides. FRIEDA enters in her nightgown, carrying a bucket of berries.

FRIEDA Is that you?

Short pause.

Your room's just the same. I kept it all the same. But there's someone in there. I hope you don't mind. A guest. He said he'd help me. Why don't you come down?

Short pause.

Henry! Come down this instant!

FRIEDA exits through the house. GEORGE comes back into the clearing.

MAS She's nuts. Talking to ghosts.

GEORGE leans the shovel back against the house and arranges the bushes to cover the hole completely.

MAS But George. Maybe if we / tried to —

GEORGE / I said I'd help her.

ACT ONE, SCENE FIVE

The next morning. GEORGE is on a ladder. He inspects the roof of the house.

MAS Nephew.

Short pause.

George. Nice view up there, huh.

Short pause.

What the hell are you doing? Making a few repairs?

GEORGE Like you said. Place is pretty rundown.

MAS So you thought you'd just fix her right up.

GEORGE I did some shingling once.

MAS Thought, I'll just do a little roofing.

GEORGE I'm helping her.

FRIEDA comes out of the house.

FRIEDA What are you doing?

GEORGE Thought I'd get a head-start on our 'restoration'. Start with your leaks.

FRIEDA You don't have to do that.

GEORGE I've done some roofing before.

FRIEDA I've had those leaks so long. This is really very kind of you. I don't know what to say.

GEORGE Do you have some tools, Frieda? A hammer, some nails?

FRIEDA Tools? Werner had lots of tools.

GEORGE Could I use them?

FRIEDA They're probably all rusty, but I could, I could probably find them. Yes. I think I know where they are. Give me a minute.

GEORGE No rush.

FRIEDA It's so nice to have someone who appreciates this place.

FRIEDA goes inside house and looks for tools.

MAS You're getting pretty sweet on that old lady.

GEORGE Uncle. Aren't you glad to just be here?

Pause.

MAS Now I get it.

GEORGE What?

MAS Ah, nephew, that's more like it!

GEORGE I don't know what you're talking about.

MAS Now I see why you're so sweet on her! Get in her good books, "oh, you're just like my grandma", maybe start talking about an offer, and then, when you move in, no more leaks.

GEORGE It's not like that.

MAS You're right, George. It's perfect. I thought you were getting soft, but really, you were way ahead of me.

GEORGE Uncle. All I'm doing is helping her out.

MAS But you would be helping her. She's right. The house should go to someone who appreciates it. Not someone who'll push everything into the ground for a condo. You'd keep it the same. That's what she wants, right?

GEORGE That's what she said.

MAS You buy the house, everyone's happy. Right?

GEORGE Right.

MAS But where are you going to get the cash?

Pause.

GEORGE I've got some money.

MAS Oh yeah?

GEORGE Dad gave it to me.

MAS Perfect!

GEORGE I want to do something good with it.

MAS Then do it! Keep doing what you were doing for three years. Educate people. You could turn this into a little museum.

GEORGE A museum.

MAS Yeah. With "historical significance".

GEORGE I don't know. I was thinking I should save the money. Dad was always riding me to give him some grandkids. So maybe someday / I could save —

MAS / kids, eh? When you don't live with your wife.

GEORGE Thanks.

MAS Where is she, anyways? Last I heard she was moving / out west —

GEORGE / she's in Vancouver.

MAS Ah.

GEORGE So what.

MAS Dirty trick, leaving you like that.

GEORGE I was never around.

MAS You were out fighting the war.

GEORGE War's over.

MAS It's never over.

GEORGE Why are we talking about Susan?

MAS You're the one who brought up the grand-kids. I'm just saying, stick to things you can get. Things you can change.

GEORGE You never let up, do you?

MAS Gotta make sure you stay on track. Look, this is something real. This is what you need. This is what we both need.

GEORGE A museum.

MAS What a great idea. Why not get it all back?

FRIEDA comes out of the house with an old tool belt.

FRIEDA I found this old thing.

MAS *(making train sounds)* Woo-woo! All you gotta do is make the offer. Hey, if you lived here, you'd be a helluva lot closer to Susan. You can almost smell the ocean, eh?

GEORGE I can fix up a few spots then go to town for some shingles. Just hand it up to me.

FRIEDA Werner just left them in the rain so much, didn't really take care of them. It will be good to use them again. I made some waffles with raspberries. Why don't you come down?

GEORGE Better to do it before it rains again.

FRIEDA Isn't it slippery? Be careful up there, Henry.

GEORGE What?

FRIEDA I said be careful up there. Come down and have a cup of coffee at least.

GEORGE All right.

GEORGE comes down the ladder.

MAS The offer, George.

GEORGE Thank you.

FRIEDA Thank you. This is — well, this is wonderful.

MAS Train's about to leave.

GEORGE The house is a lot of work for you. It's a lot to manage.

FRIEDA Yes, it's hard work, very hard, running this place. But I'm still up to it.

GEORGE I want to help you, Frieda. I told you that.

FRIEDA You're helping me already, up there, fixing the roof. And you're going to phone your committee, give the house some kind of, how do you say it, status —

GEORGE — I think I have an idea, Frieda. For a buyer.

FRIEDA A buyer?

GEORGE Me.

Short pause.

FRIEDA You? But what about your committee?

GEORGE I'd keep everything the way it is.

FRIEDA You. This is so quick.

Pause.

Well. I don't know what to say.

GEORGE It would all stay the same. Just like you said, just like we talked about. We could put it in writing.

MAS Now we're rolling, boy!

GEORGE I just have a really good feeling about the place. The location.

FRIEDA It's worth a lot of money, this land, you know. I don't know if you could afford it.

GEORGE We could talk it over with your sister —

FRIEDA — and Henry, of course. When he comes home.

GEORGE We could just start by talking.

FRIEDA So that's why you're up there looking at the roof. Is that why you offered to help me, just to butter me up —

GEORGE — Frieda, you asked me to stay. And I was looking at the roof because I wanted to do something nice for you. Really. The idea just sort of came to me, out of the blue. I wouldn't be in a rush to move in. I wouldn't push you out the door. You'd have time to make arrangements.

FRIEDA Arrangements.

GEORGE Your sister.

FRIEDA Liesel.

GEORGE She lives around here.

FRIEDA Across the river.

GEORGE We could all just talk.

FRIEDA My sister already meddles so much. I told her I wanted to do this my way.

GEORGE I want to do it your way.

FRIEDA You'd keep it the way it is.

GEORGE Better. I'd fix it up.

FRIEDA You'd have to keep a candle in the window.

GEORGE Whatever you want. Listen, Frieda, you said you wanted a buyer who appreciates this place. Well, I — really feel something here. Isn't that what you want?

FRIEDA I think so.

GEORGE Why don't you think about it. I could go to town and get some shingles.

MAS That's some slick grease, nephew. Some slick grease.

FRIEDA Henry wanted to take those tools. He was going to Israel on this program. Young Germans were helping build houses. "Shame to let those tools go to waste", he said. Werner would have none of it. He could be such a miserable man. He was in such pain. But still. If only he hadn't hurt his arm. During the war. He was building a bunkhouse. A piece of timber fell on him. He could never fix this house. He could never do anything.

Pause.

GEORGE I'll fix the place up, Frieda. I'd make the house the way it was.

FRIEDA I don't know.

GEORGE You can come back any time you want. You can go for walks, pick berries. We'll go for walks.

FRIEDA Perhaps.

GEORGE I'd refinish the wood on the inside. Replant the garden.

FRIEDA This was such a beautiful place. But you should cut the tree down. Let more light in.

MAS Hey, now.

GEORGE I'd have to think about that.

FRIEDA You can talk to my sister. She meddles. But she is a very practical woman. Her number is by the phone. Call her. Go and see her.

GEORGE You would come, too.

FRIEDA No, no, I have no head for numbers. Really, you two can work it out.

GEORGE Good. Great! Well. Here's to — new beginnings!

FRIEDA Yes. To new beginnings. You're right. This is a new beginning.

MAS You've still got the touch with the old ladies, I'll give you that.

MAS climbs up the tree.

FRIEDA I don't even know your last name.

GEORGE Oh.

GEORGE gets his card and gives it to FRIEDA.

It's Murakami.

FRIEDA Murakami. *(recognizing name)* Murakami.

GEORGE I should get up there. Before it starts raining again.

GEORGE picks up tools and climbs ladder.

FRIEDA My God. My God.

END ACT ONE

ACT TWO, SCENE ONE

The next evening. MAS still sits in the tree. GEORGE stands in the bushes.

GEORGE *(calling)* Frieda? Frieda?

MAS Wanna play some cards, George?

GEORGE I'm busy, Uncle.

MAS Lady disappeared, eh?

GEORGE I haven't seen her all day. I went out looking for her. *(calling again)* Frieda!

MAS What's the big panic?

GEORGE I'm worried, Uncle. I talked to her sister this morning. About the sale.

MAS And?

GEORGE She's very interested. We agreed on a number.

MAS Way to go, nephew.

GEORGE So we need to talk to Frieda. But she's disappeared.

MAS Sounds like trouble. I told you, never trust a white person.

GEORGE Just shut up, Uncle. I was going to call the police, but what would I say? That I'm a friend? Or, or what?

MAS Police. Those idiots don't know the trails. I coulda hid up here for days if—

GEORGE — why don't you help me? You know the trails.

MAS Can't do that, George.

GEORGE Why not.

MAS You know me. I'm more of a motivator.

GEORGE Please.

MAS All right, all right. Give me a second.

MAS descends the tree with difficulty.

Just about got stuck up here. Funny place to get stuck, eh? Considering. Cut my arms up pretty good when they hauled me out of here.

GEORGE This is ridiculous. Why am I doing this?

MAS Your grandma used to tell us a story. About those dishes. Told us it was an old Japanese legend. She probably just made it up. She'd say: Once there was this family of cranes who lived on a mountain. And one day, the mountain caught on fire. The whole family left, except one young crane, who wouldn't go. His feathers caught on fire. So he flew off to see his family, to see if they would help him. That was what was on those plates. The burning crane flying to see his family. You listening? Mom let us make up our own endings. Me, I figured he made it back. That he found his family by a lake somewhere. They poured water all over his wings, put bandages on his burns. Frank, your dad, he always said the crane just burned up, like a spark in the sky. Just died. Figured it was the crane's fault for staying and he got what he deserved.

GEORGE Dad was never into happy endings.

MAS You shoulda seen us bury those dishes. I was swearing up and down, saying I'd kill Mackenzie King. Guess what your Dad said. Nothing! Not a word. But you know, he turned away once or twice, wiping his eyes like he had dirt in them. That's the kicker, George. I knew he loved those dishes. Loved this house. And he wouldn't fight, wouldn't do anything. Goddamned Frank.

GEORGE Stop calling him that, Uncle.

FRIEDA appears out of the bushes.

Frieda! Where have you been?

FRIEDA Out for a walk.

GEORGE You've been gone for twelve hours.

FRIEDA That long? I didn't notice.

GEORGE Aren't you — aren't you hungry?

FRIEDA Oh, I had some raspberries. They are everywhere now. You can't tell where the farm ends and the forest begins.

GEORGE I talked to Liesel, Frieda. This morning.

FRIEDA Oh? How is she?

GEORGE She's very interested in the sale. I think we can work something out.

FRIEDA Where are those tools? That's how they got all rusty, just leaving them lying around. Someone could step on them, hurt themselves. I should just lock them up.

GEORGE I need them, Frieda. For the roof.

Short pause.

Liesel wants to talk, Frieda. She wants all of us to talk. She's been worried.

FRIEDA Worried!

GEORGE I was worried.

FRIEDA Really? How sweet of you.

GEORGE We need to talk about the sale.

FRIEDA We have to wait until Henry gets home. He hasn't come yet?

GEORGE No one's here. I've been here all day.

FRIEDA Well, we'll have to wait.

Short pause.

All Henry wanted to do was get away from here. He hated this place. Hated, hated, hated.

GEORGE Frieda, we need to talk. You're going to sell me the house.

FRIEDA In a minute. Don't push me. Why do you always push me?

GEORGE I'm not pushing you.

FRIEDA Why does everybody think there's something wrong with me? Liesel, now you. I'm just fine!

GEORGE All right, Frieda! I…

MAS All you want to do is talk.

GEORGE All I want to do is talk, Frieda.

MAS You're just trying to help her.

GEORGE I'm just trying to help you.

Pause.

FRIEDA I'm tired.

GEORGE You were gone a long time.

FRIEDA It felt like the last time I would see the place. I was trying to say goodbye.

GEORGE You'd always be welcome back. Whenever you wanted.

FRIEDA It wouldn't be the same.

GEORGE Frieda. It will be the same. I promise. I have plans. I want to turn it into a museum.

FRIEDA A museum?

GEORGE A kind of memorial. A tribute. To Japanese-Canadians in the area.

FRIEDA A museum! This is what you — what your committee wants?

GEORGE Well —

FRIEDA — This is what you wanted the whole time. This was all some kind of trick.

GEORGE Frieda —

FRIEDA — Let's phone your committee. I want to talk to your boss. Call him.

GEORGE Calm down.

FRIEDA You feel how wet the ground is? Memories. Soaked with them. Not all good. But mine. When I leave —

GEORGE — You take them with you.

FRIEDA No. You can't pack them in a suitcase. Some of them stay. Some of them you can't take with you.

Pause.

This was the promised land for us. A new place. Our new life.

Pause.

I can't leave.

GEORGE What do you mean?

FRIEDA I'm not leaving. I can't.

GEORGE Frieda. You're tired, you're not yourself.

FRIEDA I'm not leaving. No one can force me, not you, not Liesel. No matter what she says, how much she threatens me. Says it's her land. Her land! Did she sweat here, picking berries, raising a family? This isn't about a piece of paper. I belong here.

Pause.

I'm so tired. I'm going to bed.

GEORGE Frieda! Wait.

Pause.

This is our land.

MAS Finally!

FRIEDA Your land.

GEORGE My family's. My grandfather built this house. They lived here. They were taken away, on the train. It's ours.

MAS That's it, George! A little late, but that's it!

GEORGE My father was born here. My uncle was born here.

FRIEDA Why didn't you tell me?

GEORGE I didn't think you'd understand.

FRIEDA Understand what?

GEORGE I was afraid you'd think I was after something.

FRIEDA Aren't you?

MAS Only what's ours.

GEORGE It's not like that.

FRIEDA What's it like, then? You want the house.

GEORGE I didn't come back here expecting any of this.

FRIEDA Stop it! Stop lying! I knew.

Pause.

I knew this was your family's house. I'm not stupid. A young Jap guy comes around, wants to look around the house because he's doing "research". Wearing his best shoes to pick berries. I was sure you were here looking for something. I saw the way you looked at the place. But you said you would help. You told me about the Committee. So I trusted you. But then when you gave me your card — there is no "Committee".

Pause.

It doesn't change anything. This is my land. Not yours.

MAS I knew it.

GEORGE I'm not expecting you to just give it to me.

FRIEDA We weren't even here when your family was moved. We had nothing to do with it.

GEORGE That's not the point.

FRIEDA It wasn't just your people. There were Germans in camps in Canada, too, you know.

MAS You were never in a camp!

GEORGE *(simultaneously)* You were never in a camp. I don't think "your people" can talk about camps.

FRIEDA Am I supposed to feel guilty? Is that what you want?

GEORGE That's why I didn't tell you everything. I was trying not to pressure you.

FRIEDA You're telling me now.

GEORGE I had to, you made me.

FRIEDA Why don't you do like your father does? Just forget about it instead of blaming innocent people? Why do I always have to feel guilty?

GEORGE You told me you wanted me to buy the house. Now you're changing your mind.

Short pause.

Why don't you call Henry.

FRIEDA God, we came to this country to get away from the guilt! But no, it followed us from Meissen. It kept following me after Henry — after Werner died, and after Henry —

GEORGE — Where's Henry, Frieda.

Short pause.

Why don't you call him? Go ahead. Go inside and call him.

FRIEDA Stop it! Why are you doing this? I took you in. I didn't even know you and I invited you to stay.

GEORGE You almost killed me.

FRIEDA You said you would help me!

GEORGE Liesel told me everything, Frieda! Henry's not coming home.

Pause.

FRIEDA Some days, it's raining, and all I do is sit here. I can feel the roof sagging, water pouring through the holes. I think of Henry. I'm waiting. Then the rain lets up. There's just mist. I go walking in that mist. Maybe I see an old footprint in the mud. Maybe I imagine Henry standing right there, under that old plum tree. But that doesn't mean I'm crazy. Do you understand?

Pause.

Now Liesel wants to, to — evacuate me to a nice room somewhere, some place with a view of the mountains.

FRIEDA exits. Pause.

GEORGE *Shikataga-nai.*

MAS What are you doing?

GEORGE I'm leaving.

MAS You can't leave.

GEORGE She's not well. She's sick.

MAS Don't buy into it, George. All this stuff with her son, it's just an act.

GEORGE starts to leave.

Wait. You can't just forget about all this. You can't just forget about me.

GEORGE I can try. *Shikataga-nai*, right? I can let go.

MAS Not while I'm still around.

GEORGE I tried, Uncle. I can't do this.

MAS Where you going? Back to Winnipeg? Back to the flock?

GEORGE Yes! Back home.

MAS They'll just tell you how stupid you were, coming here. They just can't stand to see somebody do something. I used to get these letters in Angler. Stop being foolish. Stop embarrassing yourself. Your brother's got a good job at the Bay, he could find you something. Come to Winnipeg.

GEORGE They just wanted you to come home.

MAS Home!

GEORGE Where your family was.

MAS Some home! I hadn't seen them in six years! Since I was fifteen years old!

Pause.

I had nothing, not even a shirt. So I went out to Winnipeg, this big flat muddy city. And I sat at the table with them, eating A and W hamburgers, acting like nothing happened, getting married to whites, getting white jobs, smiling white smiles. Out-whiting the whites. And I could still feel this big red circle on my back. So I got up and started doing something.

GEORGE You didn't know when to stop.

MAS Your Dad. Your Dad, Frank, was the worst. Wouldn't talk to me. Wouldn't let me talk to you.

GEORGE I can't do this anymore, Uncle.

MAS The Clam King. The Chicken Shit. Goddamned Frank.

GEORGE Don't talk about him like that! Everybody's goddamned this, goddamned that. Goddamned Dad. Christ. Goddamn you, Uncle Mas! Goddamned stories stuck in my head. Dad always told me you were a trouble-maker. I never listened to him. Now look where I am. Pushing an old lady off her land. For what. For whom? Just because you turned your back on your family —

MAS — I turned my back? He turned me in! He put me in Angler. My goddamned brother. They all turned their backs on me. Except for you. At the table, I could hardly see them. They blended in so well with the white walls. This is for them. For the family. So we don't disappear.

GEORGE We won't disappear.

MAS Say you and Susan have a kid. Kid grows up sort of beige, eyes a little funny, but nobody can tell. Knows how to use chopsticks. But prefers hamburgers. But you thought about this already, right? That's why you left her.

GEORGE She left me!

MAS C'mon. You looked at your wife, and you thought about your little imaginary white kid. And then you checked the calendar for the next Redress meeting. She left you, but you were already long gone.

GEORGE I miss her.

MAS You had to do something. We both had to do something. We had to fight or disappear into the walls. We had to get something back.

GEORGE This was it. Here it was. Here it is.

MAS Exactly.

GEORGE Then why didn't you come back? If this is what you wanted, why didn't you come back?

MAS You're braver than me, George. You're the warrior. You're the only one left. The mountain's on fire.

GEORGE knocks on the door, takes the shovel and begins digging. FRIEDA comes out of the house.

GEORGE My family buried dishes here. They belong to us.

FRIEDA They're not here.

GEORGE You know about them.

FRIEDA Of course I do.

GEORGE You found them.

FRIEDA Yes, we found them. Right there, in an old rhubarb box.

GEORGE What did you do with them?

FRIEDA It was so hard, back then. We had nothing. And we found those dishes. It was like a gift from God.

GEORGE What did you do with them!

FRIEDA We needed the money so badly.

GEORGE You sold them.

FRIEDA No one would give Werner a job. They said it was his arm but I know it was because we were German. I saw the looks they gave us. What Henry had to put up with in school. The teasing, the names, even from the teachers. What were we supposed to do with them? We didn't know what had happened. We didn't know your family. Otherwise —

GEORGE — Otherwise what? You would've kept them until now?

Pause.

You knew.

FRIEDA We knew that Japanese had lost the land.

GEORGE Lost it? It wasn't something they just misplaced. The dishes were ours.

FRIEDA Don't you think I'm sorry?

GEORGE You lied to me.

FRIEDA I lied to you! I didn't pretend to be someone I wasn't.

GEORGE You were trying to use me.

FRIEDA I wanted to give you something. I wanted to make you a pie.

GEORGE Out of guilt.

FRIEDA I just wanted to give you something. But there was nothing I could give you.

MAS There's still something.

GEORGE You're right. You have nothing to give. Because it's not yours to give. It was never yours.

FRIEDA I'm not leaving.

GEORGE Yes. You are. And if Henry comes, I'll give him your new address. But somehow, I don't think I have to worry about that. He's not coming back, Frieda. That's the truth. This house is falling down. You can't handle the place. That's the truth. You just won't face it.

FRIEDA I won't face it? You're telling me about the truth? You. You con man! You trick yourself into thinking this is all something moral. You think you're all high and mighty, just because your father's family got treated badly. You think that justifies anything. Look at yourself. You're just like those people that kicked out your family. So your father's dead. Your uncle's dead. Your wife left you. Well, getting this house won't bring them back.

GEORGE Get out!

FRIEDA You get out! This is my house!

GEORGE Not for long.

FRIEDA I'm not leaving.

GEORGE It's too late.

ACT TWO, SCENE TWO

Two days later. MAS is in the tree. GEORGE enters the clearing.

MAS Hey nephew. There you are. Where'd you disappear to?

GEORGE Got a motel room.

MAS You look terrible.

GEORGE I signed the papers.

MAS It's ours?

GEORGE In a week.

MAS Way to go, nephew. I'm proud of you.

GEORGE You're proud of me.

MAS Our land, George. You bought it fair and square. 'Course, it's not those dishes. I was thinking, we could find out who they sold them to. Try to track 'em down. Whaddaya think?

GEORGE I'm tired. I can't sleep.

MAS Well, you better get some rest, cause we're going to be busy.

GEORGE We.

MAS Oh, I got a million ideas. We could — where are you going?

GEORGE goes to knock on door.

FRIEDA What? More research? Your grandmother hid her silverware in the attic? I don't think so. Are you checking up on me already? Making sure I don't set fire to the place or plant land-mines under the tree?

GEORGE I'm going to start on some projects, around the yard. Before it gets too cold.

FRIEDA One week. Do you know how hard it is to pack up a life in one week? You said you'd give me time. To make arrangements.

GEORGE I'm tired of waiting.

FRIEDA Just like all the other con men.

GEORGE: There's no one else, Frieda! Nobody wants this place. Liesel said the only other offer was a company who wanted to build a dump. She was going to level the house. I made your sister a fair offer. No, a generous offer. More than I had to.

FRIEDA It's not about the money!

GEORGE Would you rather see this place become a dump? This is what you wanted. It's not going to disappear. Look at this place. Really look at it. You can hardly keep it from falling down.

Pause.

This way you'll be near your sister.

FRIEDA My sister. Puh.

FRIEDA comes outside.

It isn't easy, you know. Keeping up a farm. I hope you don't mind if I take a bucket of your berries. *(tripping over root)* Damned tree. I wish I had cut it down years ago.

When we first came here, I would stand under that tree. I would hold Henry in my arms. And he'd reach up, with his fat little fingers, for one of the plums and I would think, thank God, we're out of Meissen. We're out of Germany. Henry will grow up fine. We're in a safe country, a good country. Canada.

GEORGE Canada!

MAS Canada, lady. I could tell you about Canada.

GEORGE: What kind of "good country" builds camps for its own people? What kind of people build camps?

FRIEDA What did Liesel tell you? What did she tell you?

Short pause.

Werner was a man with a job. That's all. He was a carpenter. He didn't know why he was building those bunkhouses. He was told it was a detention centre. That's all.

Short pause.

But Henry couldn't let it go. He couldn't erase it. He knew everything, from when he was small.

MAS He had a right to know.

GEORGE He had a right to know. You can't deny someone their past. It's not fair.

FRIEDA Fair? Henry carried that guilt around like it was his own, this giant bucket of guilt. Is that fair?

MAS You can't just clam up.

GEORGE The past isn't just yours. You can't just clam up.

FRIEDA You sound like some speech. Don't you ever get tired of it? Of the same train, going around in circles in your head?

Pause.

Well, you have it all now, don't you. This house. Your past, and your Uncle's. It all belongs to you.

FRIEDA goes back inside the house. Sound of a train whistle.

MAS Goddamned trains. Woo-woo-woo all the time.

GEORGE Why are you still here?

MAS Whaddaya mean?

GEORGE Why are you still sitting up there?

MAS I'm still having a few problems with this tree. Branches got me pretty caught. Too bad you can't help me get down.

GEORGE I am helping you. Don't you get it? I've finished your business. Now you're supposed to leave. That's the way it works.

MAS You know, I coulda hid up here for / days if —

GEORGE / hid? How could you hide?

MAS What?

GEORGE What time of the year was it? When they brought the trains?

MAS Spring. You know / that.

GEORGE / there were no leaves.

MAS So?

GEORGE They would've found you in a second.

MAS No. It was your goddamned / Dad —

GEORGE / he was trying to help you, too. You said he took the police into the trails. And where did they go?

MAS Off over there, looking for me.

GEORGE He led the police away from you.

MAS No, he / was —

GEORGE / He was giving you a chance to come down and join the family. To save face. You were scared. You were a scared little kid.

MAS I was a resister!

GEORGE Come down, Uncle.

MAS No! I like it up here. Why don't you come up, George. Damned good view from up here. You and me, we always saw eye to eye. We're here, George. Together. Just like we always wanted.

GEORGE You lied to me.

MAS We're going to make it all the same again. I was thinking, we could get the farm going again, invite people out, teach them about their roots.

FRIEDA comes out of the house. GEORGE does not see her. She watches as GEORGE talks to MAS.

GEORGE No.

MAS What's with all this, this bullshit, George. You got it all.

GEORGE I don't have anything.

MAS You've got everything! You got it back!

GEORGE I've got nothing! Susan's gone. You're gone, Uncle. This isn't the same. Dad. Dad is gone. He would barely talk to me after I started organizing meetings with you.

MAS The Clam King.

GEORGE He just wanted you — he just wanted me to forget about all of it. You can't go back, he said. He always said it would bring nothing but pain.

MAS Bullshit.

GEORGE A museum? A little history farm? Dad would've knocked it all down first.

MAS So? It's not his. It's yours.

GEORGE Do you know where I got the money? *(pulling cheque from pocket)* His Redress money. He refused to apply for it — I did it for him. And then, at his funeral, Mom just handed me this envelope. With this.

Pause.

I wanted to do something good with it! And now look what I've done. About to put a down payment on an old shack and talking to my dead uncle. Maybe, uncle, if you had the guts to come back, to see the place, to find out there's nothing here, you could've let it go. But you didn't, and now here we are. And there's nothing!

FRIEDA It doesn't help.

Pause.

It doesn't help to yell at them. I know, I've done it for years.

Pause.

Henry sent cheques. From Israel. He got work there, building memorials, houses for Jewish settlers. Sometimes with a short note, sometimes just the cheque. Werner wanted to tear the cheques up. He would go into a rage when another envelope arrived. So I started hiding them. We needed the money.

Short pause. FRIEDA takes a picture out of her pocket.

And then one day — he sent this picture. No cheque. He was standing in front of a big grapefruit tree. In the sunlight. Smiling. He was wearing one of those little black caps they wear there. He was reaching up to pick a grapefruit. My heart just raced when I saw the picture. He's coming home, I thought. He's coming home.

Pause.

So I waited. I was still waiting when you came, that day. In this rotting, cramped, cold, beautiful home.

GEORGE I just wanted the dishes.

FRIEDA Those damned dishes! If only you're uncle had taken the money, if he had just told you they weren't there.

GEORGE My uncle? What are you talking about?

MAS I never came back.

FRIEDA It was your uncle. It had to be. You said he wanted something personal.

GEORGE When did he come back?

FRIEDA In the 60's sometime.

GEORGE He never told me he came back. Why wouldn't he tell me? Is it true?

MAS I never came back!

FRIEDA Of course it's true! Why would I lie? He wrote us a letter. It was the same name. Murakami. When I saw your card, I knew.

l to r: Darcy Dunlop, Jared Matsunaga-Turnbull

photo by Trudie Lee

We offered him twenty times what they were worth. They weren't worth much, you know. It's not like we made a million dollars.

MAS She's lying, George!

FRIEDA People hold on to memories for so long. Look at you. You carry around memories that aren't even yours. You and your Uncle Frank.

GEORGE Frank?

FRIEDA You're two of a kind, he and you.

GEORGE Frank?

MAS Frank.

FRIEDA I have the letter. I looked for it the other day, when I learned your name. See, here it is.

MAS That goddamned Frank.

GEORGE Dad.

FRIEDA *(not hearing GEORGE)* Here it is. I remember his name so well, because I had just learned it in English. How it meant honest. Well, we were honest with him. We were frank. But it wasn't enough. Money wasn't enough. And we said we were sorry. We apologized over and over again.

GEORGE You offered him — money and an apology.

FRIEDA What else could we give him?

Pause. Sound of rain.

l to r: Hiro Kanagawa, Jared Matsunaga-Turnbull

photo by Trudie Lee

Rain, tree, goddamned berries. You get so used to things. Even if they hurt you. *(looking at photo again)* There was a war in Israel that year. I hope he stayed awhile in that orchard. He and Werner used to pick fruit together. I remember.

There were orchards in Meissen too. And vineyards. Miessen was very beautiful. A big castle on the Elbe. I haven't thought about that place in years. It would be good to go back.

Pause.

George.

GEORGE Yes. Frieda.

FRIEDA I really did want to make you a pie. Just because… the plums were sweet.

FRIEDA exits into the house.

ACT TWO, SCENE THREE

A week or two later. Sunshine. GEORGE is in the tree with MAS. GEORGE holds the letter. Wind chimes hang from the eaves of the house. Sound of wind chimes.

MAS You wanna play some cards?

GEORGE I wish we could.

MAS You know, you could put that letter in the museum.

GEORGE It's not going to happen, Uncle.

MAS Oh.

Pause.

So. What now.

GEORGE I think I'll spend some time in Vancouver. See the ocean.

MAS That's a good idea. We're ocean people, George.

Short pause.

Roof's looking pretty rough. Starting to sag. Winter's coming.

Short pause.

Who was that fella that came around this morning?

GEORGE Native guy. Researching old Indian camps. Left me his card.

GEORGE climbs down the tree and begins to dig.

MAS George. They're gone. The dishes are gone. You can stop now.

GEORGE I'm not looking for anything any more.

MAS What are you doing?

GEORGE This is for burying something. Don't be scared, Uncle. You can come down now.

END

Mitch Miyagawa writes and lives in Whitehorse, Yukon. He was born and raised in Edmonton, Alberta. *The Plum Tree* is his first play.